Collins

Very First
Spanish
Words

HarperCollins Publishers
Westerhill Road
Bishopbriggs
Glasgow
G64 2QT

First edition 2012

Reprint 10 9 8 7 6 5 4 3 2 1 0

© HarperCollins Publishers 2012

ISBN 978-0-00-744751-0

Collins ® is a registered trademark of
HarperCollins Publishers Limited

www.collinslanguage.com

A catalogue record for this book is available
from the British Library

Printed by Imago in China

Audio recorded and produced by
www.tomdickanddebbie.com

Artwork and design by Q2AMedia

Content developed and compiled by
Karen Jamieson

Project Management by Anna Stevenson

Translation by Sinda López Fuentes

For the publisher:
Gaëlle Amiot-Cadey
Lucy Cooper
Kerry Ferguson
Elaine Higgleton
Lisa Sutherland

This book includes a CD of Spanish words and phrases. The tracks on the CD are:

Contents

Welcome to Spain!
¡Bienvenidos a España!

Hello!
¡Hola!

Hello!
¡Hola!

What's your name?
¿Cómo te llamas?

My name is Sofía.
Yo me llamo Sofía.

Thank you.
Gracias.

You're welcome.
De nada.

Goodbye!
¡Adiós!

Goodbye!
¡Adiós!

Did you know?

At Christmas, Spanish children get their presents from the Three Kings (los Reyes Magos) on 6 January. If they are very lucky, Father Christmas usually brings them a present on Christmas Day as well!

the Sagrada Familia
la Sagrada Familia

sun
el sol

beach
la playa

tapas
las tapas

festival
la fiesta

Did you know?

In the summer, there are lots of fiestas everywhere in Spain when everyone enjoys eating, drinking and dancing together until very late, even really little children.

3

My family
Mi familia

grandpa
el abuelo

grandma
la abuela

Activities

1. Find the hidden parrot.
2. Who lives with you?

brother
el hermano

mummy
la mamá

daddy
el papá

me
yo

sister
la hermana

5

My pets
Mis mascotas

hamster
el hámster

kitten
el gatito

guinea pig
el conejillo de Indias

Activities

1. Find the hidden umbrella.
2. Can you hop like a rabbit and stretch like a cat?

tortoise
la tortuga

6

rabbit
el conejo

cat
el gato

puppy
el cachorro

dog
el perro

My day
Mi día

I get up.
Me levanto.

I get dressed.
Me visto.

I go to school.
Voy al colegio.

I play.
Juego.

Activities

1. Find the hidden kangaroo.
2. What have you done today?

I have a snack.
Como algo.

8

I listen to a story.
Escucho un cuento.

I go home.
Me voy a casa.

I have a bath.
Me baño.

I go to bed.
Me acuesto.

The weather
El tiempo

It's rainy.
Llueve.

It's snowy.
Nieva.

It's sunny.
Hace sol.

It's windy.
Hace viento.

Activities

1. Find the hidden tiger.
2. What's the weather like today?

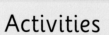

It's cloudy.
Está nublado.

It's hot.
Hace calor.

It's cold.
Hace frío.

It's stormy.
Hay tormenta.

My body and face
Mi cuerpo y mi cara

head
la cabeza

finger
el dedo

neck
el cuello

shoulder
el hombro

arm
el brazo

elbow
el codo

hand
la mano

tummy
la barriga

knee
la rodilla

foot
el pie

leg
la pierna

nails
las uñas

toe
el dedo
del pie

Activities

1. Can you pat your head and rub your tummy?
2. Can you touch your toes?

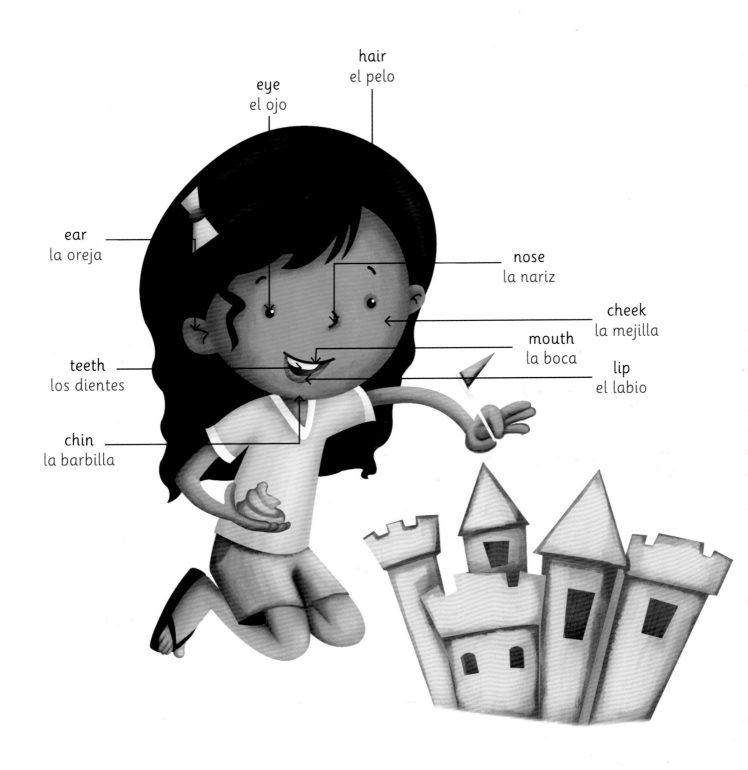

eye
el ojo

hair
el pelo

ear
la oreja

nose
la nariz

cheek
la mejilla

mouth
la boca

lip
el labio

teeth
los dientes

chin
la barbilla

13

How I feel
Cómo me siento

I'm angry.
Estoy enfadado.

I'm sad.
Estoy triste.

I'm happy.
Estoy contenta.

I'm tired.
Estoy cansada.

Activities

1. Find the hidden apple.
2. How do you feel today?

14

I'm hungry.
Tengo hambre.

I'm thirsty.
Tengo sed.

I'm scared.
Tengo miedo.

I'm shy.
Soy tímida.

Things I do
Mira lo qué hago

I stand up.
Me levanto.

I sit down.
Me siento.

I touch my toes.
Me toco los dedos de los pies.

I jump.
Salto.

Activities

1. Find the hidden teddy.
2. Mime some of these actions.

16

I eat.
Como.

I drink.
Bebo.

I cry.
Lloro.

I laugh.
Me río.

17

More things I do
Mira qué más hago

I hold my daddy's hand.
Le doy la mano a mi papá.

I wave.
Saludo con la mano.

I run.
Corro.

I walk.
Camino.

Activities

1. Find the hidden shell.
2. Can you make a noise like a monkey?

I clap.
Aplaudo.

I dance.
Bailo.

I sing.
Canto.

I make a circle.
Hago un corro.

I can count
Sé contar

1 uno

2 dos

3 tres

4 cuatro

5 cinco

Activities

1. Can you count to 10?
2. How many cars can you see in the picture?

6 seis

7 siete

8 ocho

9 nueve

10 diez

Colours
Los colores

white
blanco

green
verde

blue
azul

Activities

1. Find the hidden snake.
2. Find all the colours in the picture.

purple
morado

black
negro

brown
marrón

grey
gris

pink
rosa

red
rojo

yellow
amarillo

orange
naranja

Summer clothes
La ropa de verano

skirt
la falda

shirt
la camisa

T-shirt
la camiseta

Activities

1. Find the hidden trumpet.
2. What do you wear in summer?

swimming trunks
el bañador

swimsuit
el traje de baño

24

shorts
el pantalón corto

sandals
las sandalias

dress
el vestido

sunglasses
las gafas de sol

sun hat
el sombrero

Winter clothes
La ropa de invierno

jacket
la cazadora

boots
las botas

Activities

1. Find the hidden bicycle.
2. What do you wear in winter?

gloves
los guantes

scarf
la bufanda

coat
el abrigo

trousers
el pantalón

jeans
los vaqueros

shoes
los zapatos

hat
el gorro

sweatshirt
la sudadera

My classroom
Mi clase

teacher
la maestra

computer
el ordenador

girl
la niña

Activities

1. Find the hidden birthday cake.
2. How many children are in the picture?

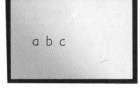

whiteboard
la pizarra blanca

schoolbag
la mochila

toys
los juguetes

poster
el póster

bookcase
la estantería

boy
el niño

book
el libro

chair
la silla

table
la mesa

pencil case
el estuche

Fast or slow?
¿Rápido o lento?

rabbit
el conejo

slow | fast
lento | rápido

tortoise
la tortuga

small | big
pequeño | grande

Activities

1. Find the hidden train.
2. Can you move slowly like a tortoise and fast like a rabbit?

hippo
el hipopótamo

strong | weak
fuerte | débil

gorilla
el gorila

dirty | clean
sucio | limpio

monkey
el mono

elephant
el elefante

Find the shapes
Busca las formas

star
la estrella

heart
el corazón

Count the shapes

Activities

1. Find the hidden mouse.
2. How many of each shape can you see in the robot?

rectangle
el rectángulo

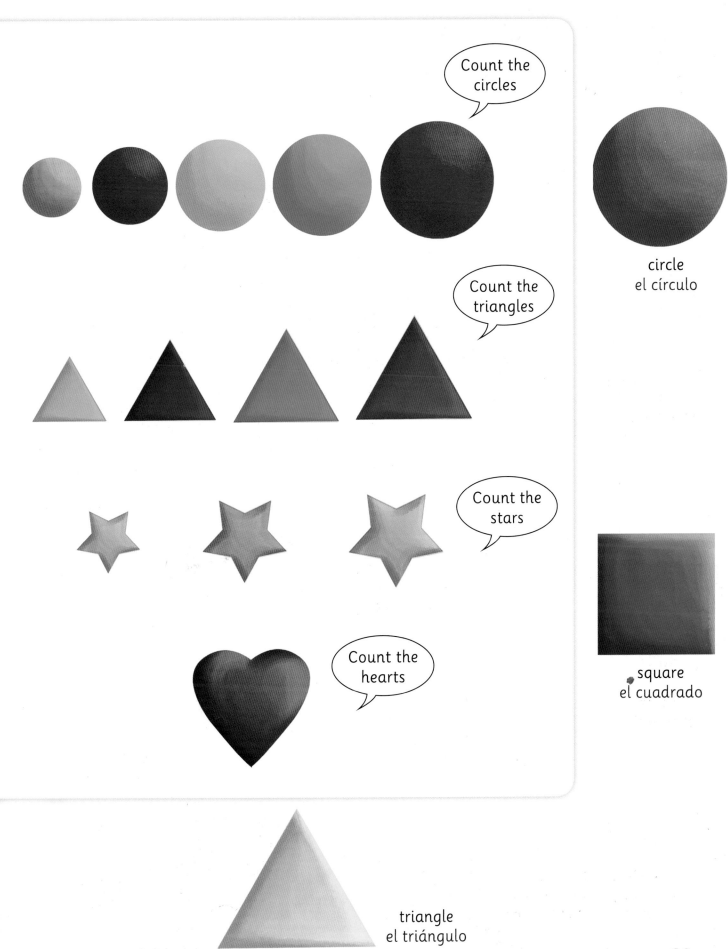

Count the circles

Count the triangles

Count the stars

Count the hearts

circle
el círculo

square
el cuadrado

triangle
el triángulo

In the sea
En el mar

dolphin
el delfín

octopus
el pulpo

seal
la foca

Activities

1. Find the hidden schoolbag.
2. How many fish can you see in the picture?

shark
el tiburón

fish
el pez

turtle
la tortuga
marina

walrus
la morsa

whale
la ballena

penguin
el pingüino

On the farm
En la granja

farmer
el granjero

straw
la paja

chicken
la gallina

Activities

1. Find the hidden octopus.
2. Can you make farm animal noises?

donkey
el burro

goose
el ganso

sheep
la oveja

mouse
el ratón

rat
la rata

duck
el pato

cow
la vaca

horse
el caballo

Animal Olympics
Las Olimpiadas de los animales

baboon
el babuino

crocodile
el cocodrilo

Activities

1. Find the hidden hat.
2. Which animal do you like best?

elephant
el elefante

zebra
la cebra

giraffe
la jirafa

rhino
el rinoceronte

hippo
el hipopótamo

lion
el león

cheetah
el guepardo

Seaside dance
El baile de la playa

shell
la concha

starfish
la estrella de mar

Activities

1. Find the hidden spoon.
2. Can you pretend to be a starfish?

jellyfish
la medusa

seahorse
el caballito de mar

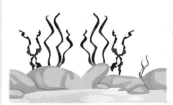

seaweed
las algas

crab
el cangrejo

rock
la roca

fish
el pez

41

At the castle
En el castillo

princess
la princesa

prince
el príncipe

dragon
el dragón

Activities

1. Find the hidden crab.
2. Can you roar like a dragon?

castle
el castillo

crown
la corona

musician
el músico

knight
el caballero

flag
la bandera

king
el rey

queen
la reina

Jungle football
El fútbol de la selva

monkey
el mono

chimpanzee
el chimpancé

snake
la serpiente

Activities

1. Find the hidden drum.
2. Can you slither like a snake?

tiger
el tigre

gorilla
el gorila

parrot
el loro

orangutan
el orangután

lizard
el lagarto

leopard
el leopardo

45

Bugs and mini beasts
Bichos e insectos

bee
la abeja

butterfly
la mariposa

Activities

1. Find the hidden bananas.
2. Can you buzz like a bee?

ladybird
la mariquita

46

grasshopper
el saltamontes

ant
la hormiga

spider
la araña

beetle
el escarabajo

caterpillar
la oruga

My birthday party
Mi fiesta de cumpleaños

birthday present
el regalo de cumpleaños

birthday card
la tarjeta de cumpleaños

ice cream
el helado

Activities

1. Find the hidden bee.
2. Can you count the candles on the cake?

balloon
el globo

birthday cake
la tarta de cumpleaños

candle
la vela

fruit
la fruta

friend
la amiga

friend
el amigo

sandwiches
los bocadillos

popcorn
las palomitas

sweets
los caramelos

water
el agua

Breakfast time
La hora del desayuno

toast
la tostada

coffee
el café

tea   cup
el té   la taza

Activities

1. Find the hidden paintbrush.
2. What do you have for breakfast?

yoghurt
el yogur

spoon
la cuchara

glass
el vaso

honey
la miel

juice
el zumo

jam
la mermelada

cereal
los cereales

milk
la leche

bread
el pan

knife
el cuchillo

My town
Mi ciudad

swimming pool
la piscina

hairdresser's
la peluquería

library
la biblioteca

school
la escuela

Activities

1. Find the hidden chimpanzee.
2. Which of these things have you seen in your town?

car
el coche

doctor's
el médico

road
la carretera

playground
el patio

motorbike
la moto

toy shop
la juguetería

supermarket
el supermercado

dentist's
el dentista

bus
el autobús

At the park
En el parque

lake
el lago

bicycle
la bicicleta

kite
la cometa

ball
el balón

Activities

1. Find the hidden tortoise.
2. Do you like to play at the park?

boat
la barca

seesaw
el balancín

54

tree
el árbol

bin
la papelera

slide
el tobogán

bird
el pájaro

scooter
el patinete

swing
el columpio

climbing frame
la torre para escalar

At the supermarket
En el supermercado

lettuce
la lechuga

mushroom
la seta

carrot
la zanahoria

Activities

1. Find the hidden train.
2. Which vegetables do you like best?

potato
la patata

broccoli
el brócoli

56

basket
la cesta

tomato
el tomate

cucumber
el pepino

red pepper
el pimiento rojo

onion
la cebolla

green pepper
el pimiento verde

The fruit stall
El puesto de la fruta

watermelon
la sandía

pear
la pera

pineapple
la piña

Activities

1. Find the hidden seahorse.
2. What is your favourite fruit?

orange
la naranja

strawberry
la fresa

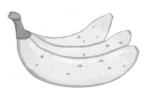

banana
el plátano

peach
el melocotón

apple
la manzana

grapes
las uvas

cherry
la cereza

In the kitchen
En la cocina

butter
la mantequilla

scales
la balanza

flour
la harina

Activities

1. Find the hidden sunglasses.
2. Do you like to help in the kitchen?

plate
el plato

honey
la miel

egg
el huevo

sugar
el azúcar

bowl
el bol

spoon
la cuchara

whisk
el batidor

oven
el horno

biscuit
la galleta

A special dinner
Una comida especial

knife
el cuchillo

rice
el arroz

fork
el tenedor

pepper
la pimienta

Activities

1. Find the hidden flower.
2. What do you like to eat for dinner?

steak
el filete

peas
los
guisantes

ketchup
el ketchup

salad
la ensalada

soup
la sopa

fish
el pescado

salt
la sal

hamburger | chips
la hamburguesa | las patatas fritas

potato | beans
la patata | las alubias

63

At bedtime
A la hora de acostarse

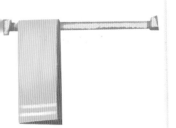

towel
la toalla

I have a shower.
Me ducho.

I dry myself.
Me seco.

I put on my pyjamas.
Me pongo el pijama.

teddy bear
el osito de peluche

I brush my teeth.
Me cepillo los dientes.

I brush my hair.
Me cepillo el pelo.

Activities

1. Find the hidden cat.
2. What time do you go to bed?

bed
la cama

64

I go to the toilet.
Voy al baño.

I wash my hands.
Me lavo las manos.

pyjamas
el pijama

I get into bed.
Me acuesto.

mirror
el espejo

I kiss my teddy.
Le doy un besito a mi osito de peluche.

I say goodnight.
Digo buenas noches.

toothpaste
la pasta de dientes

toothbrush
el cepillo de dientes

Art
El arte

paper
el papel

glue
el pegamento

Activities

1. Find the hidden rabbit.
2. How many pencils are on the table?

crayon
el lápiz de color

scissors
las tijeras

pencil
el lápiz

marker
el rotulador

paint
la pintura

brush
el pincel

Music
La música

triangle
el triángulo

guitar
la guitarra

Activities

1. Find the hidden pair of scissors.
2. Mime playing one of the instruments.

keyboard
el teclado

tambourine
la pandereta

trumpet
la trompeta

drum
el tambor

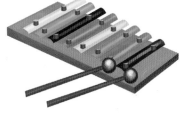

xylophone
el xilófono

violin
el violín

Let's play!
¡Juguemos!

ball
la pelota

bricks
los bloques

fire engine
el coche de
bombeross

Activities

1. Find the hidden duck.
2. What is your favourite toy?

plane
el avión

train
el tren

rocket
el cohete

doll
la muñeca

toy box
el baúl de juguetes

teddy bear
el osito de peluche

puzzle
el rompecabezas

71

Food in Spain
La cocina española

pasta
la pasta

cake
el pastel

croquettes
las croquetas

sandwich
el bocadillo

chips
las patatas fritas

With friends
Con los amigos

Activities

1. Find the hidden flower.
2. Which of these foods would you like to try?

vegetables
las verduras

chicken
el pollo

chorizo
el chorizo

cheese
el queso

lentils
las lentejas

ice cream
el helado

salad
la ensalada

paella
la paella

At home
En casa

bread
el pan

Spanish omelette
la tortilla

fish
el pescado

Words and phrases
Palabras y frases

m = masculine; f = feminine; pl = plural in Spanish only; sing = singular in Spanish only

A, a

angry: I'm angry. Estoy enfadado.
animal animal m
ant hormiga f
apple manzana f
arm brazo m
art arte m

B, b

baboon babuino m
ball (big) balón m
ball (small) pelota f
balloon globo m
banana plátano m
basket cesta f
bath: I have a bath. Me baño.
beach playa f
beans alubias f
bed cama f; I go to bed. Me acuesto.
bee abeja f
beetle escarabajo m
bicycle bicicleta f
big grande
bin papelera f
bird pájaro m
bird (large) ave m
birthday cumpleaños m
birthday cake tarta de cumpleaños f
birthday card tarjeta de cumpleaños f
birthday party fiesta de cumpleaños f
birthday present regalo de cumpleaños m
biscuit galleta f
black negro
blue azul
boat barca f
body cuerpo m

book libro m
bookcase estantería f
boots botas f
bowl bol m
boy niño m
bread pan m
breakfast desayuno m
bricks bloques m
broccoli brócoli m
brother hermano m
brown marrón
brush pincel m
bus autobús m
butter mantequilla f
butterfly mariposa f

C, c

cake pastel m
candle vela f
car coche m
carrot zanahoria f
castle castillo m
cat gato m
caterpillar oruga f
cereal cereales m pl
chair silla f
cheese queso m
cheetah guepardo m
cherry cereza f
chicken (animal) gallina f
chicken (meat) pollo m
chimpanzee chimpancé m
chin barbilla f
chips patatas fritas f
chorizo chorizo m
circle círculo m; I make a circle. Hago un corro.
clap: I clap. Aplaudo.
classroom clase f
clean limpio
climbing frame torre para escalar f
clothes ropa f

cloudy: It's cloudy. Está nublado.
coat abrigo m
coffee café m
cold: It's cold. Hace frío.
colour color m
computer ordenador m
cow vaca f
crab cangrejo m
crayon lápiz de color m
crocodile cocodrilo m
croquettes croquetas f
crown corona f
cry: I cry. Lloro.
cucumber pepino m
cup taza f

D, d

daddy papá m
dance: I dance. Bailo.
day día m
dentist dentista m
dinner comida f
dirty sucio
doctor médico m
dog perro m
doll muñeca f
dolphin delfín m
donkey burro m
dragon dragón m
dress vestido m
dressed: I get dressed. Me visto.
drink: I drink. Bebo.
drum tambor m
dry: I dry myself. Me seco.
duck pato m

E, e

ear oreja f
eat: I eat. Como.
egg huevo m
eight ocho
elephant elefante m
eye ojo m

F, f

face cara f
family familia f
farm granja f
farmer granjero m

fast rápido
festival fiesta f
finger dedo m
fire engine coche de bomberos m
fish (animal) pez m
fish (to eat) pescado m
five cinco
flag bandera m
flour harina f
foot pie m
football fútbol m
fork tenedor m
four cuatro
friend (boy) amigo m
friend (girl) amiga f
fruit fruta f

G, g

get up: I get up. Me levanto.
giraffe jirafa f
girl niña f
glass vaso m
gloves guantes m
glue pegamento m
go: I go to school. Voy al colegio.
    I go home. Me voy a casa.
goodnight: I say goodnight. Digo
    buenas noches.
goose ganso m
gorilla gorila m
grandma abuela f
grandpa abuelo m
grapes uvas f
grasshopper saltamontes m
green verde
green pepper pimiento verde m
grey gris
guinea pig conejillo de Indias m
guitar guitarra f

H, h

hair pelo m; I brush my hair.
    Me cepillo pelo.
hairdresser's peluquería f
hamburger hamburguesa f
hamster hámster m
hand mano f
happy: I'm happy. Estoy
    contenta.

hat gorro m
head cabeza f
heart corazón m
hippo hipopótamo m
hold: I hold my daddy's hand.
    Le doy la mano a mi papá.
honey miel f
horse caballo m
hot: It's hot. Hace calor.
hungry: I'm hungry. Tengo
    hambre.

I, i
ice cream helado m

J, j
jacket cazadora f
jam mermelada f
jeans vaqueros m
jellyfish medusa f
juice zumo m
jump: I jump. Salto.
jungle selva f

K, k
ketchup ketchup m
keyboard teclado m
king rey m
kiss: I kiss my teddy. Le doy un
    besito a mi osito de peluche.
kitchen cocina f
kite cometa f
kitten gatito m
knee rodilla f
knife cuchillo m
knight caballero m

L, l
ladybird mariquita f
lake lago m
laugh: I laugh. Me río.
leg pierna f
lentils lentejas f
leopard leopardo m
lettuce lechuga f
library biblioteca f
lion león m
lip labio m
listen: I listen to a story. Escucho
    un cuento.

lizard lagarto m

M, m
marker rotulador m
me yo
milk leche f
mirror espejo m
monkey mono m
motorbike moto f
mouse ratón m
mouth boca f
mummy mamá f
mushroom seta f
music música f
musician músico m

N, n
nails uñas f
neck cuello m
nine nueve
nose nariz f

O, o
octopus pulpo m
one uno
onion cebolla f
orange (colour) naranja
orange (fruit) naranja f
orangutan orangután m
oven horno m

P, p
paella paella f
paint pintura f
paper papel m
park parque m
parrot loro m
pasta pasta f
peach melocotón m
pear pera f
peas guisantes m
pencil lápiz m
pencil case estuche m
penguin pingüino m
pepper pimienta f
pet mascota f
pineapple piña f
pink rosa
plane avión m
plate plato m

play: I play. Juego.
playground patio m
popcorn palomitas f pl
poster póster m
potato patata f
prince príncipe m
princess princesa f
puppy cachorro m
purple morado
put on: I put on my pyjamas.
    Me pongo el pijama.
puzzle rompecabezas m
pyjamas pijama m sing

Q, q
queen reina f

R, r
rabbit conejo m
rainy: It's rainy. Llueve.
rat rata f
rectangle rectángulo m
red rojo
red pepper pimiento rojo m
rhino rinoceronte m
rice arroz m
road carretera f
rock roca f
rocket cohete m
ruler regla f
run: I run. Corro.

S, s
sad: I'm sad. Estoy triste.
salad ensalada f
salt sal f
sandals sandalias f
sandcastle castillo de arena m
sandwich bocadillo m
scales balanza f sing
scared: I'm scared. Tengo miedo.
scarf bufanda f
school escuela f
schoolbag mochila f
scissors tijeras f
scooter patinete m
sea mar m
seahorse caballito de mar m
seal foca f

seaweed algas f pl
seesaw balancín m
seven siete
shape forma f
shark tiburón m
sheep oveja f
shell concha f
shirt camisa f
shoes zapatos m
shorts pantalón corto m sing
shoulder hombro m
shower: I have a shower. Me ducho.
shy: I'm shy. Soy tímida.
sing: I sing. Canto.
sister hermana f
sit down: I sit down. Me siento.
six seis
skirt falda f
slide tobogán m
slow lento
small pequeño
snack: I have a snack. Como algo.
snake serpiente f
snowy: It's snowy. Nieva.
soup sopa f
Spain España f
Spanish omelette tortilla f
spider araña f
spoon cuchara f
square cuadrado m
stairs escaleras f
stand up: I stand up. Me levanto.
star estrella f
starfish estrella de mar f
steak filete m
stormy: It's stormy. Hay
    tormenta.
straw paja f
strawberry fresa f
strong fuerte
sugar azúcar m
sun sol m
sun hat sombrero m
sunglasses gafas de sol f
sunny: It's sunny. Hace sol.
supermarket supermercado m
sweatshirt sudadera f
sweets caramelos m

swimming pool piscina f
swimming trunks bañador m sing
swimsuit traje de baño m
swing columpio m

T, t
table mesa f
tambourine pandereta f
tapas tapas f
tea té m
teacher maestra f
teddy bear osito de peluche m
teeth dientes f; I brush my teeth.
    Me cepillo dientes.
ten diez
thirsty: I'm thirsty. Tengo sed.
three tres
tiger tigre m
tired: I'm tired. Estoy cansada.
toast tostada f
toe dedo del pie m
toilet: I go to the toilet. Voy al baño.
tomato tomate m
toothbrush cepillo de dientes m
toothpaste pasta de dientes f
tortoise tortuga f
touch: I touch my toes. Me toco los
    dedos de los pies.
towel toalla f
town ciudad f
toy box baúl de juguetes m
toy shop juguetería f
toys juguetes m
train tren m
tree árbol m
triangle triángulo m
trousers pantalón m sing
trumpet trompeta f

T-shirt camiseta f
tummy barriga f
turtle tortuga marina f
two dos

U, u
umbrella paraguas m

V, v
vegetables verduras f
violin violín m

W, w
walk: I walk. Camino.
walrus morsa f
wash: I wash my hands. Me
    lavo las manos.
water agua f
watermelon sandía f
wave: I wave. Saludo con la
    mano.
weak débil
weather tiempo m
whale ballena f
whisk batidor m
white blanco
whiteboard pizarra blanca f
windy: It's windy. Hace viento.

X, x
xylophone xilófono m

Y, y
yellow amarillo
yoghurt yogur m

Z, z
zebra cebra f